# Biblical Prayer Affirmations for the Supernatural

Dr. Tiffany Watkins

# Forward

"Apostle Watkins is an amazing Author, Pastor and Prophet of God that has based her life on prayer. Prayer is the most important thing in her life. She is a living Epistle of the word of God. I am looking forward to future books and materials she will release in the future!"

Archbishop Harris E. Clark

# Contents

# Introduction

Biblical Prayer Affirmations for the Supernatural combines prayer, meditation, and confession in order to manifest God's will and purpose in your life. Prayer, meditation, and confession, when combined, will affect your quality of life on earth. When we use prayer, meditation, and confession simultaneously, it affects our atmosphere in which we live.

Years ago, I created a vision and imaging book based on the word of God. In this book, it is filled with biblical prayer affirmations I have created by scripture. I often pray, meditate on, and speak out loud each affirmation relevant to my need until I see the needs come to pass.

Back on November 12, 2012, I wanted to see if prayer, meditation, and confession when combined would work for me. I decided to do a four-week experiment. In the experiment, I would do nothing but pray each day, meditate, surround myself with positive thoughts, and confess the word of God. In the first week, I decided to add fasting from food as well. I professed daily with what I desired to see God manifest in my life. The confessions and affirmations were on the Bible promises or just simply good things I desired for my life.

As a result of my 4-week personal experiment of meditation of scriptures, listening to healing music, spoken confessions over my wallet, listening to affirmations, and confession of biblical blessings, I was amazed at the results. I even decided to add an extra week to see more positive results.

After doing the experiment during this time, I received a call to do a radio interview on a previous book. I also received inspirational ideas for an infomercial business that brought in money. New orders came in for my singles book, "The Lonely Heart." I also received $2,900 total in cash gifts.

Through-out the experiment, God released these supernatural blessings to me, and I am a firm believer it works! I have found that using biblical prayer affirmations has helped me and continues to help me manifest God's will for my life. Whenever you combine prayer, meditation, and confession of God's word, there will be a stronger pull on the heavenly realm that causes the release of answered prayer, miracles, and supernatural occurrences.

My purpose in writing this book on Biblical Prayer Affirmations for the Supernatural is to help you set the right atmosphere for supernatural breakthrough and supernatural intervention. These are my very own personal prayers that God allowed me to create for my vision and imaging book.

When you begin praying these biblical prayer affirmations consistently, your atmosphere will change as mine has. Put your faith with your confession and get ready for supernatural breakthroughs, supernatural occurrences, and supernatural interventions.

As you pray these affirmations, read each one slowly while reading them out loud. Meditate on each affirmation, see yourself receiving it, and believe that it will be manifested.

# Chapter One
# Healing Affirmations

*So, you shall serve the Lord your God, and He will bless your bread and your water. And I will take sickness away from the midst of you. – Exodus 23:25*

In the beginning of human life in Eden's Garden, God's creation was perfect and whole. Sicknesses, pains and diseases were simply non-existent because man was loyal and faithful to God his Creator, He was the apple of his Creator's eyes and daily lived in His glory and presence.

Man fell for satan's temptation and sin entered into the human race bringing sicknesses, pain, and diseases along with it. We are shown in one of the most ancient books of the Bible that sickness, pains and diseases come from satan. *'So satan went out from the presence of the Lord and struck Job with painful boils from the sole of his foot to the crown of his head' – Job 2:7.*

The Lord Jesus further reveals to us that satan is the unseen personality who authored sicknesses and diseases and seeks to afflict humanity with it. *'So ought not this woman, being a daughter of Abraham, whom satan has bound…' – Luke 13:16.*

However, God's unrelenting love caused Him to provide healing for His creation. He provided His Son to take the root cause of sickness – which is sin – upon Himself and through Him, provided supernatural healing for our spirits, souls and bodies. *'Surely He has borne our griefs and carried our sorrows; Yet we esteemed Him stricken, smitten by God and afflicted. But He was wounded for our transgressions, He was bruised for our iniquities; The chastisement for our peace was upon Him, and by His stripes we are healed' – Isaiah 53:4,5.*

God in His love has provided supernatural healing and divine health for those who serve Jesus and expects us to receive healing by faith and to enjoy divine health by obedience to His laws.    Let these healing prayer affirmations bring divine healing into your life.

# Healing Prayer Affirmations

"Father, the woman with the issue of blood in Mark 5:28-29; 34 touched the hem of your garment, and immediately the fountain of her blood dried up. I thank you that you have done the same for me, and any sickness lingering in my body has dried up according to your word."

"Because I have set my love upon you, therefore you will deliver me, Father. You will set me on high because you know my name. I am calling upon you, and you are possessing my healing and answering me. You are with me in trouble. You are delivering and honoring me. With long life, you are satisfying me, and you are showing me your salvation, according to Psalm 91:14-16."

"God, I thank you that you have sent your word, healed me, and delivered me from my destructions according to Psalm 107:20."

"Just as you told the Israelites in Jeremiah 30:17 that you would restore health to them and heal them of their wounds, Father, I thank you that you are restoring my health and healing me of my wounds."

"Father, just like it was said in Job 33:25 that his flesh shall be fresher than a child's; he shall return to the days of his youth and it was so, I thank you that my sickness of _____(fill in the sickness) and you have made my flesh fresher than a child's. I have returned to the days of my youth."

"Jesus, you went about all the cities and villages preaching the gospel of the kingdom and healing every sickness and every disease among the people according to Matthew 9:35. I thank you, Jesus, for the gospel of the Kingdom healing me of every sickness and disease in my body."

"Lord, you said to those who fear your name that the Sun of Righteousness shall arise with healing in His wings. I shall go out and grow fat like stall-fed calves. Lord, I thank you for the Sun of Righteousness arising over me with healing in His wings so that I am healed and can go and grow in the name of Jesus, according to Malachi 4:2."

"In Psalm 107:19-20 God, you healed those who cried out to you in trouble. You healed them out of their distresses, sent your word, healed, and delivered them from their destructions. God, I thank you for healing me of my distresses, sending your word to me, healing me, and delivering me from my destructions."

"Jesus, by your stripes, I am healed because you bore my sin in your body on the tree that I may die to sin and live for righteousness according to 1 Peter 2:24."

"Jesus, you were able to cause the blind to see, the lame to walk, the lepers to be cleansed, and the dead raised. All the multitudes that followed you were healed. According to Matthew 11:5, I declare and receive your healing for me in Jesus' name!"

"Lord, I fear you, and I am departing from evil, and you said this will be health to my flesh and strength to my bones. My body is healthy, and my bones are strengthened in Jesus' name according to Proverbs 3:5-8."

"Jesus, in Mark 6:56, you entered into the cities and villages and saw the sick in the marketplace. As many as you touched, they were all made well. I thank you for touching me and making me well."

"Psalm 147:3 says, 'He healeth the broken in heart, and bindeth up their wounds.' I thank you that I am healed of my broken heart, you have bound up my wounds. God, I no longer hold on to the hurt and know that your hands have mended my heart."

"3rd John 1:2 says, 'Beloved, I wish above all things that thou mayest prosper and be in health, even as thy soul prospereth.' I am prospering in my soul, my health, and every area of my life."

# Chapter Two
# Angelic Visitation
# Affirmations

*I sought the Lord, and He heard me, and delivered me from all my fears. They looked to Him and were radiant and their faces were not ashamed. The angel of the Lord encamps around those who fear Him, and delivers them – Psalm 34:4,5,7*

Behold what manner of love the Father has bestowed on us, that we should be called children of God (1 John 3:1). Father God's love is simply comparable to none, in that His original design of creation entails angelic protection and assistance for all His children.

You are not designed to live in fear of the insecurity and violence in the world today because you have the Father's angels available to you, as God has commissioned them to take good care of His saints. However, many people are yet to experience angelic protection or assistance in their whole lives for one reason or the other.

Here's a few helpful tips to increase your chances of experiencing the angelic:

- Develop a close and consistent walk with God, as God is only committed to those who are committed to Him. Do your best to spend personal time alone with God on a very regular basis thus helping yourself to get more aligned with His ways (See James 4:8).

- Have regular times of prayer. A prayerless Christian will hardly experience angelic help because God's word shows us that God will commit His angels especially to those who are given to prayer (See Psalm 91:1-4,9-12). Besides, angels are naturally attracted to those who regularly worship God in prayer. This played out in the life of Cornelius, a man given to prayer, when the Lord's angel appeared to him unexpectedly (See Acts 10:1-4).

- Always be full of thanksgiving and praise, even when you are going through unpleasant situations. People who complain never get to experience God's presence or His angels. When God's children find themselves in a difficult situation and they begin to bless the name of the Lord, they are most likely to encounter angelic deliverance or assistance (See Daniel 3:26-28).

- Pray for the release of angelic intervention in your life.

# Angelic visitation Affirmations

"Father in Genesis 28:12-13, Jacob had a dream in which he saw a stairway resting on earth with its top reaching to heaven. The Angels of God were ascending and descending on it, and you revealed to him that you would give him and his descendants the land he was lying on. So, Father, I thank you for an open gateway to heaven in my life for the Angels of God to ascend and descend before me. Reveal to me the land you have given me and the instructions on how to carry it out."

"God, according to Genesis 18:1-3; 10, 14, you sent three Angels to Abraham by the Oak of Mamre to deliver the promise of Isaac, and you showed them favor. I thank you that you are sending your angels to me in order to deliver the promised seed of purpose in my life."

"Father, in Exodus 23:20-22, you told Moses you sent an Angel before him in order to guard him along the way and to bring him to the place for which you had prepared for him. I thank you for sending an Angel before me to guard me along my way and to bring me to the place you have prepared for me".

"God, I thank you that, according to Psalm 91:11-12, the angel of the Lord encamps around about me because I fear you. They deliver me out of every stressful situation and those things that are impossible for me to accomplish on my own."

"Father, in Acts 8:26-40, the angel of the Lord visited Philip and told him to go south to Gaza in order to minister salvation to an Ethiopian eunuch. Thank you for sending the angel of the Lord to me with directions and instructions on how to lead others to salvation. I thank you for the salvation of sinners taking place around me and in my church."

"Father, we see in Acts 27:23 that the angel of the Lord stood by Paul telling him not to fear because God would save him and those on the ship during the storm. Lord, I thank you for sending angels by me to encourage me during my storms in life just as you did for Paul."

"In my times of weakness, God has sent his angels to me just like He did for Elijah in 2 Kings 19:5-8 to strengthen me and feed me back to energy. I will continue to complete the work God has ordained for me to accomplish."

"God, I thank you for opening my eyes to see the victory in the spiritual realm just like you did for Elisha's servant in 2 Kings 6:17. Open my eyes to see who is on my side."

"God, just like you sent an angel of the Lord to Joseph in order to let him know Mary's pregnancy was from the Lord, do it for me. Send your angels to me to confirm what is truly from you that I may see what you have for me, according to Matthew 1:20.

"Psalm 91:11 says, he will give his angels charge over thee, to keep thee in all thy ways." God, I thank you that there are angels all around to protect me when I go in and when I go out. They will protect me wherever I go."


"God, just as the angel of the Lord visited Mary and Joseph to tell them not to fear because they brought good tidings of great joy, send those angels to me. Manifest the same good tidings of joy that was in Luke 2:10. Release good news to me that will make me and everyone around me happy."

# Chapter Three
# The Blood Affirmations

*And they overcame him by the blood of the Lamb – Revelation 12:11*

The blood of Jesus is a double-sided weapon; it is a very potent and offensive weapon against the devil and likewise a defensive one for the believer. It is one of the mysteries of Christ's kingdom given to His people. Its first mention and application was in the book of Exodus where God reveals this mystery to Moses. '*Then Moses called for all the elders of Israel and said to them, "Pick out and take lambs for yourselves according to your families and kill the Passover lamb. And you shall take a bunch of hyssop, dip it in the blood that is in the basin, and strike the lintel and the two doorposts with the blood that is in the basin. – Exodus 12:23.* The New Testament makes it clearer for us and shows us that Jesus is the Lamb of God whose blood protected the Israelites back then (See John 1:29, 1 Corinthians 5:7, 1 Peter 1:18-21, Revelation 5:6-9). These bible passages further reveal that *now* the blood of the Lamb is for the whole world – including every tribe, tongue and family. Therefore, it is no more limited to the people of Israel.

Now what does the blood do for us?

- The blood covers our sins and cleanses us from its effects. It washes us and makes us acceptable to God our Father. It cleanses our conscience so we can stand blameless before God (See Colossians 1:14,21-22).

- The blood silences our accuser every time he attempts to accuse us before God our loving Father (See Revelation 12:10,11).

- The blood commands the respect of both God's angels and satan's demons. It protects us from destruction, plagues, demonic attacks and makes us immune to the hideous operations of the kingdom of darkness (See Exodus 12:13).

However, we must learn to regularly apply the blood by faith – through speaking it with our mouths – for us to enjoy its amazing power and benefits.

# The Blood Affirmation Prayers

"Father, I thank you that the blood of Jesus is on me, and because you see your blood on me, no plague shall be upon me to destroy me, according to Exodus 12:13. I apply the blood over my house, and God will see the blood and pass over my door just like he did in Exodus 12:23. He will not allow the destroyer to enter my house and strike me down."

"I thank you, Father, that Jesus loves me and washed me from my sins in his own blood, according to Revelations 1:5."

"I overcome Satan by the blood of the Lamb and the word of my testimony according to Revelations 12:11. I have an overcoming spirit by the blood of the Lamb. I overcome all traps set by the enemy over my life."

"I thank you, Father, that the blood of Jesus Christ cleanses me from all sins according to 1 John 1:7."

Father, I thank you that the blood of Christ, who through the eternal spirit offered himself without spot to God, has purged my conscience from dead works to serve the living God according to Hebrews 9:14. I am now serving the Kingdom of God with a renewed mind!

"I have the boldness to enter into the holiest of holies by the blood of Jesus by a new and living way that you have consecrated for us, through the veil, that is his flesh, according to Hebrews 10:19-20. Jesus, your blood has made me whole."

"Father, I thank you that I am redeemed through your blood, and I am made nigh by the blood of Christ according to Ephesians 1:7; 2:13. Your blood draws me close to you, and I hear your voice."

"Ephesians 1:7 says, we have redemption through Jesus' blood, the forgiveness of sins, according to the riches of his grace. Therefore, I refuse to feel guilty about what God has forgiven me for. I repent of all my sins and receive the riches of his grace."

"I am justified by your blood, according to Romans 5:9 and I am saved from God's wrath."

# Chapter Four
# Word Of
# Knowledge/Wisdom
# Affirmations

*But the manifestation of the Spirit is given to each one for the profit of all: for to one is given the word of wisdom through the Spirit, to another the word of knowledge through the same Spirit – 1 Corinthians 12:7,8.*

The Spirit of God gives us spiritual gifts as sons of God, in order to prove to the world, the reality of God's existence and to demonstrate His unsearchable wisdom, deep knowledge and unmatchable power.

A believer who is gifted with the word of knowledge is an instrument to prove that God knows all things in the past and in the present; On the other hand, one who is gifted with the word of wisdom is an instrument to prove that

God knows [and is able to determine] the future even before it comes.

The gift of the word of knowledge is important in our lives as it is useful in giving us accurate information of the past and present. This gift was employed by Jesus Christ to tell a [formerly unbelieving] woman of her past and present life, eventually leading to her repentance and salvation (See John 4:16-19, Luke 1:36). This gift can also reveal the identity of people and expose hidden thoughts of the heart (See John 1:41-42, John 2:24-25).

The gift of the word of wisdom reveals the future and tells a future event that is going to happen to an individual or a particular place. We see this gift manifesting in the life of Agabus, who warned Paul of dangers ahead of him (See Acts 21:10,11). This gift is useful in warning us of future dangers, exposing the plans of the devil (See Luke 22:31,32).

It is also useful in unveiling to us God's plan for our future, preparing us for a future blessing, thereby increasing our level of confidence and faith in God (See Judges 13:2-5).

# Word of knowledge/wisdom

# affirmations

"I am seeing with God's eyes, and he helps me to see the knowledge he has preserved for me. He has caused me to walk in great prosperity and spiritual discernment, according to Proverbs 22:12."

"I know your desire for every situation in my life. I have the spiritual eye to see what is of God and what is from Satan. I know when good is present and when evil is present. This discernment leads me into blessings and helps me to avoid those things which are harmful to my life."

"Father I thank you that you are opening up my eyes to receive your wisdom that allows me to partake in Hebrews 4:12-13 which says, For the word of God is quick, and powerful, and sharper than any two-edged sword, piercing even to the dividing asunder of soul and spirit, and of the joints and marrow, and is a discerner of the thoughts and intents of the heart. Neither is there any creature that is not manifest in his sight: but all things are naked and opened unto the eyes of him with whom we have to do. I receive the spirit of this scripture into my heart, soul, mind, and I absorb it in every bone of my body in Jesus' name. Father, allow me to see as you see and hear as you hear. God, I thank you for revealing those hidden things I cannot see."

"I have the eye to see false prophets because you said in Matthew 7:15-20 to beware of false prophets which come to you in sheep's clothing. Inwardly, they are ravening wolves. I shall know them by their fruits. I will not be deceived."

"God, I thank you that the eyes of my heart are enlightened that I may know the hope to which you have called me, the riches of your glorious inheritance in the saints. I thank you that I know what the exceeding greatness of the working of your mighty power is according to Ephesians 1:18-19. My mind is open to the truth. I know the blessings God has promised me. I am experiencing your great power in the earth."

"God, I thank you, according to Isaiah 50:4-5, that you have given me the tongue of the learned that I may know how to speak a word in season to him that is weary. You awaken me every morning. You awaken my ear to hear as the learned. The Lord God hath opened my ear, and I am not rebellious, neither have I turned back. I know what to say at the right time. I hear you every morning and know what to do."

"Father, I accept your words and store up your commands within me. I turn my ear to wisdom and apply my heart to understanding. I call out for insight and cry aloud for wisdom. I look for this wisdom like silver and search for it like hidden treasure, according to Proverbs 2:1-15. I now understand the fear of the Lord and find the knowledge of God. I receive wisdom, knowledge, and understanding from God's mouth. God has victory in store for me."

"God, I thank you that you are a shield to me and guard my course and protect me. I understand what is right, just, fair, and see every good path. I thank you that wisdom is entering my heart, and knowledge is pleasant to my soul. Discretion is protecting me, and understanding is guarding me. Wisdom is saving me from wicked men, men whose words are perverse, and those that leave the straight path to walk into darkness. God is protecting me from those who delight in doing wrong and rejoice in the perverseness of evil. I stay away from those whose paths are crooked and devious in their ways, according to Proverbs 2:1-15."

"My love abounds more and more in the knowledge and depth of insight so that I may be able to discern what is best. I am pure and blameless until the day of Christ. I am filled with the fruit of righteousness that comes through Jesus Christ for the glory and praise of God, according to Philippians 1:9-10."

"Father, I pray that you may strengthen me out of your glorious riches with power through your spirit in my inner being. Christ dwells in my heart through faith. Christ has rooted and grounded me in love so that I may have power together with the saints. This power I have with the saints causes me to grasp how wide, long, high, and deep the love of Christ is. God reveals to me the love that surpasses all knowledge, and I am filled to the measure with all the fullness of God according to Ephesians 3:16-21. God is doing immeasurably more than I can ask, think, or imagine according to his power that is at work in me.

"The Spirit of the Lord rests upon me. The spirit of wisdom, understanding, counsel, power, knowledge, and the fear of the Lord rests upon me. I will not judge by what I see with my eyes or decide by what I hear with my physical ears only, according to Isaiah 11:2-3. I will judge with God's eyes and hear with God's ears."

"Father, be with my mouth and teach me what I should say just like you told Moses you would do in Exodus 4:12." Thank you for teaching me what I am to say in order to bring deliverance to me and those around me."

# Chapter Five
# Wealth Affirmation Prayers

*Again proclaim, saying, 'Thus says the LORD of hosts: "My cities shall again spread out through prosperity; The LORD will again comfort Zion, and will again choose Jerusalem.' – Zechariah 1:17*

There is nothing God does without a reason. God prospers His people primarily for the advancement of His kingdom. It is not so that we can drive the costliest cars, neither is it so that we can be elites in our society and be named among the wealthiest in our society.

God has a kingdom, and through His Church, He seeks to dominate the earth with His love, power and wisdom. He wants His people to win His lost creation back to Him. He wants us to show His compassion for the poor and the needy by bringing them out of their hopeless situations (See Proverbs 19:17) which is possible only when His people prosper financially.

Here's what God said to Abraham, *'I will make you a great nation; I will bless you and make your name great; And you shall be a blessing.' – Genesis 12:2.* Abraham was truly a blessing to many people, even strangers and tired travelers (See Genesis 18:2-5). He equipped his servants with his own resources and went to rescue multitudes of captives from their captors (See Genesis 14:13-16).

All true Christians are seeds of Abraham and inheritors of the Genesis 12:2 promise (See Galatians 3:29). However, not all would [automatically] experience financial prosperity except those who determine to be selfless, sacrificial and diligent in their service to God and humanity. Although the blood of Christ makes financial prosperity available to us (2 Corinthians 2:8,9), we are solely responsible for what we make out of it.


God prospers us for sharing with others and distributing to His kingdom purpose and not just for selfish possession (See 1 Peter 4:10, 1 Timothy 6:17-19).

# WEALTH AFFIRMATION PRAYERS

"God, I thank you that the prayer of Moses manifests in my life from Deuteronomy 1:11. You are our God, and may Adonai, the God of my ancestors, increase me yet a thousand-fold and bless me as you have promised."

"God, I remember Adonai my God because it is you who gives me the power to get wealth. You are confirming your covenant which you swore to my ancestors as it is happening even today, according to Deuteronomy 8:18."

"Father, the psalmist says in Psalm 37:25-26, I have been young; now I am old, yet not once have I seen the righteous abandoned or his descendants begging for bread. All-day long, you are generous and lend, and your descendants are blessed. God, I thank you that you will never abandon me nor leave me begging for bread, but you are blessing me so much that I am able to lend to others. Everyone that will come from my physical and spiritual loins shall be blessed."

"Father, Psalm 85:12 says, Adonai will also grant prosperity; our land will yield its harvest. I ask that you grant me prosperity, and I decree that my land is yielding its harvest now! I speak that my money is coming forth, my blessings are coming forth, and my harvest is coming forth. I am walking in abundant prosperity and unlimited harvest."

"Father, Psalm 115:12-16 says, Adonai has kept us in mind, and he will bless us! He will bless those that fear him. May Adonai increase my numbers; may I be blessed by Adonai, the maker of heaven and earth. Heaven belongs to Adonai, but the earth he has given to humankind. God, I thank you that you are increasing my numbers financially in my personal bank account. I thank you that you have given me everything that belongs to me. All goodness has been given to me, and I receive all that your goodness has to offer."

Father, Ecclesiastes 11:1 says, cast my bread upon the waters: for I shall find it after many days. The complete Jewish version says to send my resources out over the seas, and eventually, I will reap a return. So, Father, I thank you that I am finding my seed now and reaping a return now. I thank you that as I give, it is returning to me, and there is no lack between my giving and receiving in Jesus' name! I am finding the blessings from the money I have given. I am finding the blessing from the time I have sown in helping others. My money has found me, and I am able to give more to help others."

"Father, Proverbs 11:25 says, the generous soul will be made rich, and he who waters will also be watered himself. The Complete Jewish Version says, the person who blesses others will prosper, he who satisfies others will be satisfied himself. Lord, I thank you that because of my generous ways, you are prospering and satisfying me. I have blessed others, and now you are blessing me!"

"Father, you said in Malachi 3:10-12 to bring all of the tithes into the storehouse, that there may be food in your house. You commanded us to try you now and see if you would not open the windows of heaven for us and pour out blessings for us that we won't even have room enough to receive. You promised to rebuke the devourer for our sake so that the devil will not destroy the fruit of our ground. Nor shall the vine fail to bear fruit for me in the field, says the Lord of hosts. Therefore, God, I bring all my tithes into the storehouse and thank you for opening the windows of heaven over my life. You are pouring me out so many blessings that I don't even have room enough to receive! The devourer has been rebuked on my behalf! The nations call me blessed, and I am a delightful land."

"Proverbs 10:24 says the desire of the righteous shall be granted. Therefore, I thank you, God, for answering my desire to be wealthy. This wealth will not only bless me but bless others around me and allow me to build your Kingdom."

"God, I thank you that Philippians 4:19 says, and my God will supply every need of mine according to your riches in glory in Christ Jesus. I thank you that you are now supplying every one of my financial, spiritual, and emotional needs. Do it according to your riches in glory, which is abundant and unlimited! Shower your glory upon me now because I know when your glory comes, your riches follow."

"Father, in Psalm 1, you said the blessed ones who reject the advice of the wicked will be like a tree planted by the streams. They bear fruit in season, and their leaves never wither. You said everything they do succeeds. Father, I don't take the advice of the wicked. Therefore, I am like a tree planted by the streams. I bear fruit in season; my leaves never wither, and everything I do succeeds in Jesus' name!"

"Proverbs 28:25 says he who trusts in Adonai will prosper. Because I trust in you, Lord, I prosper in every area of my life."

"God, you promised the children of Israel in Deuteronomy 28:12-13 that you would open for them your good treasure, do the same for me. Let the sky give my land its rain at the right seasons and bless everything I undertake. I will lend unto many nations and not borrow. You will make me the head and not the tail. I will be above in everything and come out on top."

"The Lord is my shepherd; I shall not want according to Psalm 23:1-3! Everything I need you are manifesting it now as I pray. You make me to lie down in green pastures. I am at rest and not in distress. You lead me beside the still waters, and I am at peace with every situation in my life. You restore my soul from all that I have given out. You lead me in the paths of righteousness for your name's sake so that I am never led in the wrong direction."

"God, I thank you that every day you are loading me with benefits according to Psalm 68:19." Nothing but good comes my way."

"I thank you, God, that you are taking care of me and not allowing my soul to famish according to Proverbs 10:3." Everything about me is full and overflowing by God's grace."

"Because I fear the Lord and delight greatly in his commandments according to Psalm 112:1-3, wealth and riches are in my house: and my righteousness endures forever. My seed shall be mighty upon the earth. I am the generation of the upright, and I am blessed."

"3 John 2 says you wish above all things that we prosper and be in good health even as our souls prosper. I decree and declare that I am prospering, walking in good health, and my soul is prospering."

"Father, you said in Proverbs 11:24, there is he that scattereth and yet increaseth. The complete Jewish version says some give freely and still get richer. I thank you that as I continue to scatter my seed, you are increasing me on every side! The more I give, the richer I get. Daily I am getting richer!"

"For the Lord has blessed me with favor. You have compassed me with a shield, according to Psalm 5:12."

"Proverbs 12:14 says a man shall be satisfied with good by the fruit of his mouth, and the recompense of a man's hand shall be rendered to him. Father, I thank you that whatever I put my hands to do, I shall prosper and be rewarded."

"Proverbs 13:22 says a good man leaveth an inheritance to his children's children, and the wealth of the sinner is laid up for the just. Father, I thank you for opening doors for the sinner's wealth to come to me. All the wealth that the sinner has for me is being released now. My bank accounts are full and overflowing."

"I am walking in the overflow, and everything around me is being multiplied as in Mark 8:1-9. God, take what I have and cause an overflow to remain. I am walking in the thousand-fold blessing.  You are taking the little in my life and making it much in Jesus' name."


"All of my bills are paid in full, and the blessings of the Lord are upon my life.  Jesus, I thank you for making a way for me to pay all my debt like you did in Matthew 17:27.  I thank you for leading me to my catch that will allow me to be debt-free."

# Chapter Six
# Holy Spirit Visitation
# Affirmations

―――――〜―――――

*Then the churches throughout all Judea, Galilee and Samaria had*
*peace and were edified. And walking in the fear of the Lord and in*
*the comfort of the Holy Spirit, they were multiplied – Acts 9:31*

The Holy Spirit, whom Jesus sent to the earth after His
ascension to heaven, has many roles to play in the
Church and in the life of every individual believer. He
is our teacher, our comforter, our guide, a revealer of
hidden things and our strengthener (See John 14:16-26,
John 15:26, John 16:7-15).

One of His major roles in the Christian's life is to help him
pray effectively. He does this in two ways: by teaching us
the principles of prayer in the word of God, and then by
quickening and strengthening our spirits to pray as we
should, despite our weakness and ignorance. *Likewise the*
*Spirit also helps in our weaknesses. For we do not know what we*

*should pray for as we ought, but the Spirit Himself makes intercession for us with groanings which cannot be uttered – Romans 8:26.*

He knows what we need more than we do, and so He waits and longs for us to seek His guidance over every issue of concern, to cast our cares on Him, and to yield our spirits to Him when we pray. It is important for us to know the Holy Spirit as intimately as we can, because He is all-knowing and all-seeing. Praying correctly and getting answers to our prayers are both easier when we are sensitive to the gentle nudgings and instructions of the Holy Spirit. It is likewise important for us to develop and keep building our faith, because we cannot get answers to our prayers without faith (See James 1:6,7).

# HOLY SPIRIT VISITATION AFFIRMATIONS

"John 16:13-15 says, Howbeit when he, the Spirit of truth, is come, he will guide you into all truth: for he shall not speak of himself; but whatsoever he shall hear, that shall he speak: and he will shew you things to come. He shall glorify me: for he shall receive of mine and shall shew it unto you. All things that the Father hath are mine: therefore, said I, that he shall take of mine, and shall shew it unto you. Holy Spirit will guide me into all truth in all areas of my life. Reveal to me the thoughts of God when it comes to my life and those I must witness to. My ears are open to hear the voice of God, and my eyes are capable of seeing through the eyes of God."

"Father, I ask for the leading of the Holy Spirit to assist me in every endeavor that I take because you promised this in Luke 11:13. You asked, if we then being evil know how to give good gifts to our children: how much more shall our heavenly Father give the Holy Spirit to them that ask him? I thank you for the supernatural manifestation of your Holy Spirit to assist me whenever assistance is needed."

"Acts 4:31 says when the apostles prayed, they were filled with the Holy Ghost and continued to speak the word of God with boldness. Thank you, Lord, for filling me with the gift of the Holy Ghost. You are helping me to preach the word of God with boldness. Thank you, Holy Ghost, for your presence being with me to boldly proclaim the gospel."

"John 14:26 says, But the Helper, the Holy Spirit, whom the Father will send in Jesus name', will teach me all things and bring all things to my remembrance regarding what Jesus has said to me. God, reveal to me, by the Holy Spirit, what Jesus has said to me."

"Romans 8:26 says, likewise, the Spirit helps us in our weakness. For we do not know what to pray for as we ought, but the Spirit himself intercedes for us with groanings too deep for words. Therefore, Holy Spirit help me to know how and what to pray for in every situation."

"Father, Jesus, your son, said in John 14:16-17 that he will pray to you, and you shall give us another Comforter, that he may abide with us forever. Even the Spirit of truth; whom the world cannot receive, because it seeth him not, neither knoweth him; but we know him; for he dwelleth with us and shall be in us. So,

Father, allow the comforter to be with me and abide with me forever! Let the comforter walk with me and continually remain with me. Make him visible in my everyday life."

"It says in 1 Corinthians 2:9-10 but as it is written, eye hath not seen, nor ear heard, neither have entered into the heart of man, the things which God hath prepared for them that love him. But God hath revealed them unto us by his Spirit: for the Spirit searcheth all things, yea, the deep things of God. Holy Spirit reveal to me what God has in store for me and my ministry. Reveal to me the direction I am to take in life. Reveal to me the deep things of God in order to help me prosper spiritually, financially, emotionally, and physically."

"May I abound in and be filled with the fruit of righteousness that comes through Jesus Christ, according to Philippians 1:11."


"For his divine power has been bestowed upon me, all things that are suited to life and Godliness, through the full knowledge of him who called us by and to his own glory and excellence according to 2 Peter 1:3."

# Chapter Seven
# Miracles, Signs and Wonders.

―――――⁓―――――

*God also bearing witness both with signs and wonders, with various miracles and gifts of the Holy Spirit, according to His own will –
Hebrews 2:4 NKJV*

Miracles, signs and wonders are divine attestations to the reality of God's kingdom on earth and are ordained by God to be the experience and lifestyle of His people in all generations. The operations and the will of God are transgenerational and does not end with just one generation (See Psalm 78:1-7). Therefore, it is His will for Christians to walk in supernatural power right from the birth of the church in the book of Acts till the very time the church will be taken up from the earth (See 1 Thessalonians 4:15-17).

Jesus, in the days of His earthly ministry, demonstrated His power by performing miracles, signs and wonders. He healed sicknesses and diseases supernaturally (See Matthew 4:24), He cast out demons (See Matthew 9:32-33), He multiplied food (See Matthew 14:16-21), and He raised the dead (See John 11:40-44).

The Holy Spirit is the power of God, by Whom Jesus was able to perform miracles, signs and wonders (See Luke 1:35). The same Holy Spirit is in the church today, and He is able to empower His people to walk in the supernatural like Jesus did, because 'as He is, so are we in this world' – 1 John 4:17.

We are called to be His witnesses by showing God's love, power and glory to the world. We can only achieve this through the power and wisdom of the Spirit of Jesus (See John 14:12). Jesus desires that His church would walk in the power of the Holy Spirit and bring salvation, healing and deliverance to the multitudes of the earth.

The Great Commission of making disciples of all the people of the earth, baptizing and teaching them to observe God's Word can only be fulfilled when we walk in the fullness of Christ's supernatural power, and to this end Jesus says, 'I am with you always even to the end of the age'. – Matthew 28:20.

# Miracles, signs, and wonders

# affirmations

"Father, be with me like you were with Joshua, the priests, and men of war in Joshua 6:20-25. Cause every wall to fall flat in my life that has been constructed by the enemy. Allow me to take the city and destroy the works of Satan by your blood. Be with me as you were with Joshua. Dismantle every 'Jericho-like fortress' set up to keep me out of my promised blessings."

"Lord, bless me just like you did for the widow in 1 Kings 17:7-15. She had only a handful of flour in a jar and a little olive oil in a jug, but you blessed her. As I serve you, let there be an endless supply of blessings in my life. Take the little I have and do not let it be used up nor run dry. Send rain on every place of drought in my life. Let there be food every day for me and my family. Never let my jar of blessings be used up nor the oil for the anointing run dry in my life."

"Father, do in my life what you allowed Elisha to do in 2 Kings 2:19-22. If there is anything in my life that is causing death to my purpose, death to my family, or causing me to have miscarriages in the spirit, heal it now. Heal everything in my life so that it would never again cause death or make my life unproductive."

"There will be no more interruption of destiny concerning my life."

"Because I've accepted Jesus into my life, miracles are a normal occurrence for me."

"Signs of God's presence follow me as I profess His Word."

"God, I thank you that you are the God who performs miracles, and you display your power among me and the people according to Psalm 77:1."

"And the glory of the Lord shall be revealed unto me and those around me, and all flesh shall see it together; for the mouth of the Lord has spoken it according to Isaiah 40:5. I thank you for revealing your glory to me in a new way that I may experience your presence and power as I've never experienced before."

"Manifest Isaiah 58:8 in my life as I fast so that my light shall break forth like the morning, and my healing shall spring forth speedily; my righteousness shall go before me, and the glory of the Lord shall be my rear guard. Thank you for giving me the power of a new life, peace, and prosperity."

"Be exalted O God above the heavens, according to Psalm 57:5. Let your glory be over my life and over all the earth."

"But my horn shalt thou exalt like the horn of a unicorn: I shall be anointed with fresh oil, and this oil shall transform my life with new zeal according to Psalm 92:11. I have a new determination to walk in God's supernatural power that causes me to sit in heavenly places with Christ Jesus."

"Because I've accepted Jesus into my life, I have access to the Heavens. My citizenship is in Heaven according to Philippians 3:20, therefore, I have legal right to confess and receive all His word says about me."

"Jesus, in Mark 8:22-26, you healed the blind man in Bethsaida so that his physical sight returned. He was able to see clearly again. I ask in Jesus' name that my spiritual sight be healed so that I can see clearly in the heavenly realm. I believe I will see Angels, have heavenly encounters, and see with x-ray vision into the mind of God. The veil has been lifted, and my eyes are now opened."

"God, just like you did unusual and extraordinary miracles by the hands of Paul according to Acts 19:11, do unusual and extraordinary miracles by my hands in your own wonderful way through me."

"Father allow my preaching to be accompanied with the power of the Holy Spirit just as Paul's ministry was. In Romans 15:19, Paul's ministry was accompanied with the power of miracles, signs, wonders, and all of it by the power of the Holy Spirit. I decree and declare that the Holy Spirit follows my life with signs, miracles, and wonders as I follow Christ."

"Whenever there is an attack on my life, God will work his signs and wonders on my behalf as he said in Daniel 6:27. God will deliver me from the power of the lion as he did for Daniel. No attack will take me out. God is my savior and my deliverer. He will work signs and wonders in heaven and earth on my behalf. I will be free to fulfill his purposes for my life."

"Every day I experience a new level of His glory through dreams and visions."

"Father, just like you sent a sound to David of marching in the tops of balsam trees thank you for sending me a sound to gain victory over every defeat in my life. You did this for David in 2 Samuel 5:23-25 and you will also do this for me. My ears are open to hearing and ready to walk in my place of victory!"

# ABOUT THE AUTHOR

***"And we know that all things work together for good to them that love God, to them who are the called according to his purpose…"***

Tiffany Watkins is a certified Chaplain, Life Coach and author who was born and raised in South Carolina and attended Lander University, Greenwood, where she attained a Bachelor of Science in Sociology/Child and Family Studies. She has also received her Master's in Divinity and her Doctorate in Biblical Counseling. She lives with her cat, Cookie, and has a niece and 2 nephews whom she adores.

Since then she has gained numerous other qualifications and is currently Pastor of Renewed Faith Ministries, while also being linked to several other fellowships and community groups.

Tiffany's other great passion in life is for writing and she has linked this with her own life and through her work in the church, to date having authored 2 books, **Sexual Abuse of Youth Within the Church** and **The Lonely Heart: A Guide to Successful Single Living**.

In her free time Tiffany loves to travel and is slowly but surely ticking off each US state, with her ambition to visit them all currently at the halfway stage. She is also keenly interested in philanthropy and was a part of the Young Philanthropist Program of United Way in 2017-2018, serving her community through regular volunteering and service.

In the future, Tiffany sees her role as saving lives, relieving suffering and helping to maintain human dignity through humanitarian work.

You can contact or follow Tiffany Watkins at

**Amazon:** amazon.com/author/doctortiffany

**Twitter:** https://twitter.com/tifflove44

**Facebook:**
https://www.facebook.com/tiffany.watkins.5686

**Email address**: pastorwatkins@bellsouth.net

**Website:** www.renewedfaithministriesinc.com

**Blog:**
https://www.goodreads.com/author/show/4036270.Tiffany_Watkins/blog

www.ingramcontent.com/pod-product-compliance
Lightning Source LLC
Chambersburg PA
CBHW071931020426
42331CB00010B/2818